A Simple
Garden Journal

James Cramer
& A Simple Life
Magazine

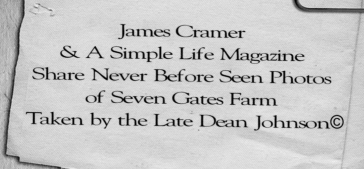

James Cramer
& A Simple Life Magazine
Share Never Before Seen Photos
of Seven Gates Farm
Taken by the Late Dean Johnson©

A Simple Garden Journal
A Seasonal Journal
& Planner for your Garden

I want to thank my dear friend Jimmie Cramer for entrusting me with these amazing photographs from Dean Johnson. I felt close to Dean while working on this project. I love you, Jimmie, and I am so thankful we found each other.

_____
_____
_____
_____
_____
_____
_____
_____
_____
_____
_____
_____
_____
_____
_____
_____
_____
_____
_____
_____
_____
_____
_____
_____
_____
_____
_____

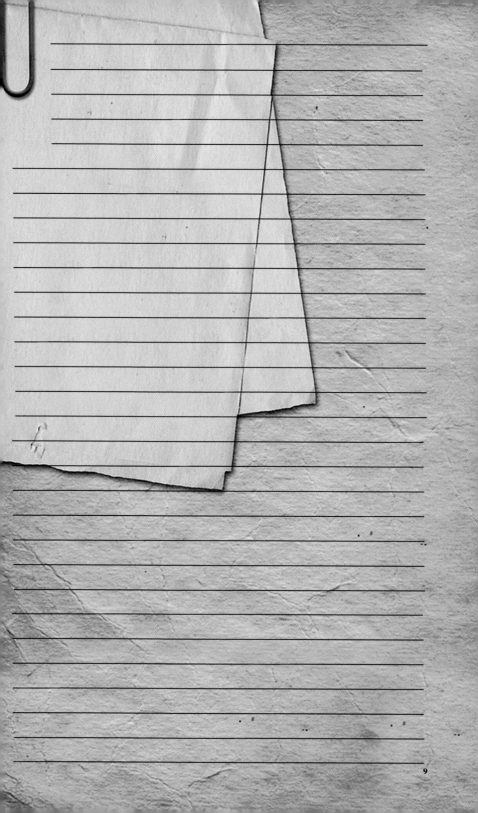

"In my garden there is a
large place for
sentiment. My garden
of flowers is also my
garden of thoughts and
dreams. The thoughts
grow as freely as the
flowers, and the dreams
are as beautiful."
                    -Abram L. Urban

Spring Gardening Checklist

The garden is beginning to wake up and all the dreams you had in the Winter are ready to be put into action!

March
~Prepare your soil beds.
~Buy seeds, compost, new tools etc.
~Build raised garden beds.

April
~Sow seeds - some in the greenhouse, and some can go outside.
~Ready your plant beds for planting - begin planting your early plants.

May
~Everything should be planted by mid-May.
~Water new plants and net your fruit trees.
~Spring is the time to plant vegetables such as onions, potatoes and some varieties of lettuce.

PERENNIAL WISH LIST

ANNUAL WISH LIST

"Don't judge each day by the harvest you reap but by the seeds that you plant."
~Robert Louis Stevenson

PLANTING DATES

Last Frost Date —————————————————

Date —————————————————
Planted —————————————————

—————————————————
—————————————————
—————————————————

Date —————————————————
Planted —————————————————

—————————————————
—————————————————
—————————————————

Date —————————————————
Planted —————————————————

—————————————————
—————————————————
—————————————————

Date —————————————————
Planted —————————————————

—————————————————
—————————————————
—————————————————

Date —————————————————
Planted —————————————————

—————————————————
—————————————————
—————————————————

PLANTING DATES

Last Frost Date _____

Date _____

Planted _____

_____

_____

_____

Date _____

Planted _____

_____

_____

_____

Date _____

Planted _____

_____

_____

Date _____

Planted _____

_____

_____

_____

Date _____

Planted _____

_____

_____

_____

PLANTING DATES

Last Frost Date ———————————————————

Date ———————————————————
Planted ———————————————————
———————————————————
———————————————————
———————————————————

Date ———————————————————
Planted ———————————————————
———————————————————
———————————————————
———————————————————

Date ———————————————————
Planted ———————————————————
———————————————————
———————————————————
———————————————————

Date ———————————————————
Planted ———————————————————
———————————————————
———————————————————
———————————————————

Date ———————————————————
Planted ———————————————————
———————————————————
———————————————————
———————————————————

PLANTING DATES

Last Frost Date ——————————————————

Date ——————————————————

Planted ——————————————————

——————————————————

——————————————————

——————————————————

Date ——————————————————

Planted ——————————————————

——————————————————

——————————————————

——————————————————

Date ——————————————————

Planted ——————————————————

——————————————————

——————————————————

——————————————————

Date ——————————————————

Planted ——————————————————

——————————————————

——————————————————

——————————————————

Date ——————————————————

Planted ——————————————————

——————————————————

——————————————————

——————————————————

"To see a world
in a grain of sand
and heaven in a
wildflower,
Hold infinity in the
palm of your hand,
and eternity in an hour."

-William Blake

What Is Growing & Blooming

Date _____

_____

_____

_____

_____

Date _____

_____

_____

_____

_____

Date _____

_____

_____

_____

_____

Date _____

_____

_____

_____

_____

Date _____

_____

_____

_____

_____

What Is Growing & Blooming

Date _____

_____

_____

_____

_____

Date _____

_____

_____

_____

_____

Date _____

_____

_____

_____

_____

Date _____

_____

_____

_____

_____

Date _____

_____

_____

_____

_____

What Is Growing & Blooming

Date _____

_____

_____

_____

_____

Date _____

_____

_____

_____

_____

Date _____

_____

_____

_____

Date _____

_____

_____

_____

_____

Date _____

_____

_____

_____

_____

Nature does nothing useless. —Aristotle

Plants & Their Meanings - A Liberty Garden

1. Sweet Bay – glory
2. Rosemary – for remembrance
3. Lemon thyme – activity, bravery, courage & strength
4. Southernwood - constancy
5. Santolina – wards off evil
6. Rue – clear vision, grace
7. Clary sage – clear vision
8. Bergamot (bee balm) - compassion, empathy
9. Lemon verbena - enchantment
10. Calendula – grief, despair
11. Peppermint – wisdom
12. Lemon balm – sympathy, rejuvenation
13. Apple mint - love, immortality
14. Sage – immortality
15. Nasturtium – patriotism, victory in battle
16. Bronze fennel – strength
17. Heirloom rose – victory, pride
18. Coltsfoot – justice
19. Lady's mantle – comfort, protection
20. Daisy – hope
21. Soapwort – cleanliness
22. Hyssop – cleanliness
23. Purple coneflower - life
24. Comfrey – healing
25. Wormwood – absence
26. Garlic – healing
27. Horehound – health
28. Yarrow – health
29. Borage – courage
30. Scented geranium - unity

The Dog Days of Summer ...

_____

_____

_____

_____

_____

_____

_____

_____

_____

_____

_____

_____

_____

_____

_____

_____

_____

_____

_____

_____

_____

_____

_____

_____

_____

_____

_____

_____

_____

_____

_____

_____

Summer Gardening Checklist

Summer is the time to enjoy the fruits of your labor. Flowers are in bloom, vegetables are ready to can, fruit is ready to be picked, and herbs are ready to be dried.

June
~Weed and Water. Begin harvesting and using herbs.

July
~Sow Winter greens and lettuce in trays.
~Deadhead flowers.
~Thin plants to give them better air circulation and exposure to the sun.
~Harvest ripe vegetables and fruits as soon as possible to stay a step ahead of pests.

August
~Prepare beds for Winter vegetables.
~Prune dead flowers.

"Love is to the heart what the summer is to the farmer's year. It brings to harvest all the loveliest flowers of the soul."

- Billy Graham

Favorite Plants to Remember

Name _____

Where Purchased _____

Variety _____

Bloom Time _____

Water Frequency _____

Name _____

Where Purchased _____

Variety _____

Bloom Time _____

Water Frequency _____

Name _____

Where Purchased _____

Variety _____

Bloom Time _____

Water Frequency _____

Name _____

Where Purchased _____

Variety _____

Bloom Time _____

Water Frequency _____

Favorite Plants to Remember

Name _____

Where Purchased _____

Variety _____

Bloom Time _____

Water Frequency _____

Name _____

Where Purchased _____

Variety _____

Bloom Time _____

Water Frequency _____

Name _____

Where Purchased _____

Variety _____

Bloom Time _____

Water Frequency _____

Name _____

Where Purchased _____

Variety _____

Bloom Time _____

Water Frequency _____

Favorite Plants to Remember

Name _____

Where Purchased _____

Variety _____

Bloom Time _____

Water Frequency _____

_____

Name _____

Where Purchased _____

Variety _____

Bloom Time _____

Water Frequency _____

_____

Name _____

Where Purchased _____

Variety _____

Bloom Time _____

Water Frequency _____

_____

Name _____

Where Purchased _____

Variety _____

Bloom Time _____

Water Frequency _____

_____

Pest & Disease Problems

Date —————————————————————————

Plant Type ———————————————————————

Problem ————————————————————————

Solution ————————————————————————

————————————————————————————

————————————————————————————

Date —————————————————————————

Plant Type ———————————————————————

Problem ————————————————————————

Solution ————————————————————————

————————————————————————————

————————————————————————————

Date —————————————————————————

Plant Type ———————————————————————

Problem ————————————————————————

Solution ————————————————————————

————————————————————————————

————————————————————————————

Date —————————————————————————

Plant Type ———————————————————————

Problem ————————————————————————

Solution ————————————————————————

————————————————————————————

————————————————————————————

Pest & Disease Problems

Date

Plant Type

Problem

Solution

Date

Plant Type

Problem

Solution

Date

Plant Type

Problem

Solution

Date

Plant Type

Problem

Solution

" Though I do not believe that
a plant will spring up where no
seed has been, I have great faith
in a seed. Convince me that you
have a seed there, and I am
prepared to expect wonders."

- Henry David Thoreau

The Love of Fall ...

_____

_____

_____

_____

_____

_____

_____

_____

_____

_____

_____

_____

_____

_____

_____

_____

_____

_____

_____

_____

_____

_____

_____

_____

_____

_____

_____

_____

_____

_____

Fall Gardening Checklist

Although the gardens are asleep, there is still plenty of work to keep the avid gardener busy.

September
~Plant perennials, shrubs and trees.
~Take care of weeds now before they flower and leave more seeds.
~Pick the last of your tomatoes and let them ripen inside.

October
~All crops should be harvested before the frost.
~Rake leaves.
~Watch pumpkins and squash for mice invasion.
~Plant spring-flowering bulbs, all the way up until the ground freezes.

November
~Prune trees and bushes.
~Hoe beds to aerate the soil.
~Plant spring bulbs.

"Love the trees until their leaves fall off, then encourage them to try again next year."

~Chad Sugg

November comes
And November goes,
With the last red berries
And the first white snows.

With night coming early,
And dawn coming late,
And ice in the bucket
And frost by the gate.

The fires burn
And the kettles sing,
And earth sinks to rest
Until next spring.

-Clyde Watson

Winter Gardening Checklist

Winter is a time for gardeners to dream of warmer, longer days. Pore over your seed catalogs and envision your new garden plots.

December
~Cut holly, cedar, balsam, and evergreens for your holiday decorating. Create wreaths and roping to adorn your home indoors with fresh greens from your garden.

January
~Prune trees, shrubs, roses.
~Repair and maintain any structures such as fences, gates, greenhouses, garden sheds etc.
~Do maintenance and repairs on your machinery.

February
~Remove all dead plants.
~Protect your winter vegetables with cloches, plastic tents, etc.
~Provide cover for tender and early-flowering plants. Place a circle of stakes around them and drape cloth covers so as not to touch their leaves.

"When the snow is still
blowing against the
window-pane in January
and February and the
wild winds are howling
without, what pleasure
it is to plan for summer
that is to be."
                          -Celia Thaxter

SEED CATALOGS

Name _____

Phone _____

Website _____

Notes _____

_____

_____

Name _____

Phone _____

Website _____

Notes _____

_____

_____

Name _____

Phone _____

Website _____

Notes _____

_____

_____

Name _____

Phone _____

Website _____

Notes _____

_____

_____

SEED CATALOGS

Name _____

Phone _____

Website _____

Notes _____

_____

_____

Name _____

Phone _____

Website _____

Notes _____

_____

_____

Name _____

Phone _____

Website _____

Notes _____

_____

_____

Name _____

Phone _____

Website _____

Notes _____

_____

_____

SEED CATALOGS

Name _____

Phone _____

Website _____

Notes _____

_____

_____

Name _____

Phone _____

Website _____

Notes _____

_____

_____

Name _____

Phone _____

Website _____

Notes _____

_____

_____

Name _____

Phone _____

Website _____

Notes _____

_____

_____